The Ketchup Cookbook

Cooking with Ketchup: So Much More than a Condiment!

BY

Christina Tosch

Copyright 2020 Christina Tosch

Copyright Notes

This Book may not be reproduced, in part or in whole, without explicit permission and agreement by the Author by any means. This includes but is not limited to print, electronic media, scanning, photocopying or file sharing.

The Author has made every effort to ensure accuracy of information in the Book but assumes no responsibility should personal or commercial damage arise in the case of misinterpretation or misunderstanding. All suggestions, instructions and guidelines expressed in the Book are meant for informational purposes only, and the Reader assumes any and all risk when following said information.

Table of Contents

Introduction 7

Appetizers Lite Bites 9

    Antipasto 10

    Beef and Vegetable Soup 12

    Butterscotch Chicken Wings 14

    Cornflake Crusted Bacon Strips 18

    Country-Style Ribs 20

    Deviled Eggs 22

    Ginger Glazed Beef Kabobs 24

    Mini Hawaiian Burgers 27

    Mini-Meatballs 30

    Prawn Cocktail 34

    Shrimp Pasta Salad 38

Toasted Reubens 41

Mains... 44

BBQ Mac n' Cheese.. 45

Catfish Stew 48

Chickpea Ketchup Curry... 51

Cola Chicken 54

Crab Hash 57

Grilled Lamb Chops with Pineapple 60

Japanese-Style Ketchup Spaghetti 63

Ketchup Shrimp... 67

Meatloaf 70

Root Beer Glazed Chicken.. 73

Shepherd's Pie 75

Slow Cooker Pork Chops 78

Sweet and Savory Brisket 80

Teriyaki Salmon with Ketchup 82

Sauces, Dips 'n Sides 85

Baked Beans 86

Burger Sauce 88

Caramelized Garlic and Onion Ketchup 90

Catalina Dressing 92

Comeback Sauce 94

Curry Ketchup 96

Honey Apple Barbecue Sauce 98

Hot Reuben Dip 100

North Carolina Red Coleslaw 103

Pineapple and Brown Sugar BBQ Sauce 106

Red Remoulade 109

Spiced Cranberry Ketchup 111

Strawberry Ketchup 113

Sweet and Sour Sauce 115

Author's Afterthoughts 117

About the Author 118

Introduction

While today ketchup is mainly a table condiment, this didn't happen until the 1900s with the advent of French fries, hot dogs, and hamburgers. Before then, ketchup was a popular ingredient for pies and sauces.

It's now time to ketchup on some fun and fascinating facts.

- A staggering 97 percent of homes in American have ketchup in their kitchen cupboards
- Every year the nation celebrates National Ketchup Day on June 5th

- People were cooking with ketchup as far back as the 18th century with ketchup recipes appearing in American and British cookbooks
- Each person eats approximately three bottles of ketchup every year
- In Asia, cooking with ketchup is the norm, and it is often used as an ingredient for sweet and sour sauce
- If you eat four tablespoons of ketchup, your body is getting the same nutritional value as it does from a medium-size fresh tomato
- The acid in ketchup can restore pots and pans to their former glory by removing any tarnish
- In 1876 thanks to the F J Heinz Company ketchup went on sale to the public
- USA President Donald Trump takes his steak well-done with a side of…you guessed it, ketchup!

The Ketchup Cookbook features 40 recipes that will show you how to use this store-cupboard staple as a key ingredient for all sorts of savory dishes.

Appetizers, lite-bites, mains, dips, sauces, and sides all taste better when you are cooking with ketchup.

Ketchup is so much more than a condiment!

Appetizers Lite Bites

Antipasto

Appetizers don't come much simpler than this! You can either buy store-bought Catalina Dressing or make your own.

Servings: 20

Total Time: 1hour 15mins

Ingredients:

- 1 cup fresh mushrooms (sliced)
- 1 cup small-size cauliflower florets
- 1 cup red peppers (chopped)
- 1 onion (peeled, chopped)
- 1 cup tomato ketchup
- 1 cup Catalina dressing (any brand, or see recipe in Chapter 1)
- ½ cup black olives (peeled, sliced)
- Crackers (to serve)

Directions:

1. Add the mushrooms, cauliflower, red peppers, onion, ketchup, and dressing to a pan and bring to a boil before simmering on moderate-low heat for 15 minutes. You will need to stir occasionally until thickened.

2. Remove the pan for the heat and stir in the olives. Set aside to cool.

3. When sufficiently cooled, transfer to the fridge for half an hour before serving.

4. Serve with crackers.

Beef and Vegetable Soup

So next time you are catering for a crowd, why not prepare this hearty soup featuring meat and vegetables? It makes a perfect lunchtime lite bite.

Servings: 12

Total Time: 1hours 25mins

Ingredients:

- 1 quart canned tomatoes
- 2 (14 ounce) cans mixed vegetables
- ½ medium cabbage (shredded)
- 1 cup tomato ketchup
- 1 tbsp salt
- 1-2 tbsp black pepper
- 1 pound ground beef
- 1 medium-size onion (peeled, chopped)

Directions:

1. Add the canned tomatoes to a large saucepan.

2. Without draining, add the mixed veggies to the pan, followed by the cabbage, ketchup, salt, and black pepper.

3. In a frying pan, brown the beef. Add the onion to the pan and cook until golden.

4. Transfer the beef and onion mixture, undrained to the large saucepan, and bring to boil for 2-3 minutes.

5. Reduce the heat to moderate and cover with a tight-fitting lid.

6. Simmer for 60 minutes and serve.

Butterscotch Chicken Wings

Ketchup is ideal for including in a marinade, its sticky consistency is perfect and it adds tang to sweet ingredients.

Servings: 20

Total Time: 55mins

Ingredients:

- 2 pounds chicken wings
- Nonstick cooking spray

Marinade:

- 2 tbsp soy sauce
- 2 tbsp ketchup
- 2 tbsp Sriracha chili sauce
- 1 tsp pepper
- 1 tsp crushed red pepper flakes
- 1 tsp onion powder
- ½ tsp salt

Butterscotch Sauce:

- ½ cup sugar
- ½ cup 2% milk (warmed)
- 2 tbsp butter

Crumb Topping:

- 1 tbsp butter
- ½ cup panko breadcrumbs
- 2 green onions (diagonally sliced, divided)
- 1 garlic clove (peeled, minced)
- ½ tsp salt
- ½ tsp pepper
- 2 red bird's eye chili peppers (sliced)

Directions:

1. Preheat the main oven to 400 degrees F.

2. With a sharp knife, cut through the 2 wing joints and discard the wingtips.

3. For the marinade: In a bowl, combine the soy sauce, ketchup, chili sauce, pepper, red pepper flakes, onion powder and salt. Add the wings and toss until evenly and well coated.

4. Using aluminum foil, line a 15x10" pan and grease with nonstick cooking spray.

5. Bake the wings in the prepared baking pan for 10 minutes before turning the heat down to 350 degrees and baking for 12-15 minutes, until the juices run clear.

6. Remove the wings from the oven and keep warm.

7. In the meantime, in a small frying pan, spread the sugar and without stirring cook over moderate heat until it starts to melt.

8. Drag the melted sugar to the middle of the pan so that it evenly melts.

9. Without stirring, cook until the sugar turns an amber color.

10. Stir in the warm milk along with the butter, and while frequently stirring simmer for 5-7 minutes, until thickened. Keep warm.

11. In a large frying pan over moderate heat, melt the butter. Add the breadcrumbs to the butter along with 1 green onion, garlic, salt, and black pepper. Cook while stirring until the breadcrumbs are golden, for approximately 2 minutes. Put to one side.

12. When you are ready to serve, toss the chicken wings in the butterscotch sauce.

13. Scatter with the crumb topping, remaining onion, and sliced peppers.

14. Serve and enjoy.

Cornflake Crusted Bacon Strips

Crisp strips of bacon, coated in ketchup and cornflakes, are a quick and easy appetizer to serve with beer, wine, or soda.

Servings: 10

Total Time: 45mins

Ingredients:

- ½ cup evaporated milk
- 2 tbsp ketchup
- 1 tbsp Worcestershire sauce
- Dash of pepper
- 20 strips of bacon
- 1 cup cornflakes (crushed)

Directions:

1. Preheat the main oven to 375 degrees F.

2. In a large-size bowl, combine the milk with the ketchup, Worcestershire sauce, and pepper.

3. Add the strips of bacon, turning to coat evenly.

4. Dip the strips of bacon into the crushed cornflakes, while gently patting to make sure the coating adheres.

5. Arrange the bacon on 2 wire racks. Position each rack on an ungreased 15x10x1" baking pan.

6. Bake in the oven until golden and crispy, rotating the pans halfway through cooking, for 25-30 minutes.

7. Serve.

Country-Style Ribs

Tuck into these sweet and tangy country-style pork ribs. They make an amazing appetizer.

Servings: 4

Total Time: 5hours 30mins

Ingredients:

- 1½ cups ketchup
- ½ cup packed brown sugar
- ½ cup white vinegar
- 2 tsp seasoned salt
- ½ tsp liquid smoke
- 2 pounds boneless country-style pork ribs

Directions:

1. In a slow cooker of 3-quart capacity, combine the ketchup with the brown sugar, white vinegar, seasoned salt, and liquid smoke.

2. Add the ribs to the slow cooker and turn to evenly coat.

3. Cover and cook on low until the meat is tender, for 5-6 hours.

4. Transfer the pork to a serving platter. Skim off any fat from the cooking liquid.

5. Transfer to a small pan to thicken, bring to boil, and cook until the sauce is reduced to 1½ cups; this will take 12-15 minutes.

6. Serve the sauce with the ribs.

Deviled Eggs

These deviled eggs are a tasty blast for the past.

Servings: 12

Total Time: 30mins

Ingredients:

- 6 hard-boiled eggs (shelled)
- 3 tbsp mayonnaise
- 1-2 tbsp ketchup
- 1 tsp vinegar
- ½ tsp mustard
- ¼ tsp salt
- Paprika (to garnish)

Directions:

1. Cut the eggs in half lengthwise and gently scoop out the yolks. Set the egg white halves to one side.

2. In a food blender or processor, combine the yolks with the mayonnaise, ketchup, vinegar, mustard, and salt.

3. Spoon the filling into the holes in the egg white.

4. Garnish with paprika and place in the fridge to chill before serving.

Ginger Glazed Beef Kabobs

Kabobs will always be a popular appetizer or lite bite. They are easy to prepare and ready in less than half an hour.

Servings: 6

Total Time: 25mins

Ingredients:

- 1½ pounds boneless beef sirloin steak (cut into 1" pieces)
- 12 small-medium mushrooms
- 2 bell peppers (1 red and 1 green, cut into 1" chunks)
- 1 cup tomato ketchup
- ¼ cup dry sherry
- 1 tbsp ginger root (peeled, minced)
- 1 tbsp honey
- 1 tbsp Worcestershire sauce
- 2 tsp lite soy sauce
- 2 green onions (finely sliced)

Directions:

1. First, soak 6 wooden skewers for half an hour before using.

2. Thread the steak, mushrooms, and bell peppers alternately onto the skewers.

3. In a bowl, combine the remaining ingredients (ketchup, dry sherry, ginger root, honey, Worcestershire sauce, and soy sauce and stir until entirely blended. Set half of the mixture to one side.

4. Grill the kabobs for 10-12 minutes, while occasionally turning and until the meat is cooked to a medium level of doneness. Brush with half of the sauce during the final 2-3 minutes of grilling.

5. Transfer the kabobs to a serving platter and garnish with onions.

6. Serve the kabobs with the remaining ketchup mixture.

7. Enjoy.

Mini Hawaiian Burgers

These delicious mini burgers are bursting with tropical flavor thanks to sweet, juicy pineapple.

Servings: 12

Total Time: 1hour 5mins

Ingredients:

- 1 (8 ounce) can unsweetened crushed pineapple
- 1 green onion (finely chopped)
- 1 tsp Worcestershire sauce
- ½ tsp salt
- ½ tsp garlic powder
- ½ tsp salt-free seasoning blend
- ½ tsp pepper
- 1 pound ground turkey
- ½ pound uncooked chorizo sausage
- ⅔ cup ketchup
- 12 Hawaiian sweet rolls (split)
- 6 lettuce leaves (cut in half)
- 12 slices tomato

Directions:

1. First, drain the pineapple and set ½ a cup of juice to one side.

2. In a large bowl, combine the pineapple with the green onion, Worcestershire sauce, salt, garlic powder, salt-free seasoning blend, and pepper.

3. Add the ground turkey and chorizo and lightly mix until thoroughly combined.

4. Shape the mixture into 12 (½" thick) patties.

5. Place the patties on a broiler pan and cook for 4-5 minutes on each side, approximately 4" away from the heat source. The burgers are sufficiently cooked when they register an internal temperature of 165 degrees F.

6. In the meantime, in a bowl, combine the ketchup with the pineapple juice, set aside early.

7. Serve the burgers inside the toasted rolls along with the lettuce, and tomatoes, and ketchup mixture.

Mini-Meatballs

Pop-in-the-mouth perfection, these sticky and sweet mini meatballs will have everyone asking for the recipe.

Servings: 4-6

Total Time: 45mins

Ingredients:

- 10½ ounces minced pork
- 1 ounce soft breadcrumbs
- 1 tbsp parsley (chopped)
- 1 small-size red onion (peeled, finely diced)
- 2 tbsp Parmesan (freshly grated)
- 1 egg (lightly beaten)
- Sunflower oil (for cooking)

Glaze:

- 5 tbsp tomato ketchup
- 1 garlic clove (peeled, crushed)
- 2 tsp smokey paprika
- 1 tbsp soy sauce
- 1 tbsp sherry vinegar
- 1 tbsp butter
- 1 tbsp soft brown sugar
- Special Equipment:
- 24 cocktail sticks

Directions:

1. Preheat the main oven to 375 degrees f.

2. In a bowl, combine the minced pork with the breadcrumbs, parsley, onion, and Parmesan cheese. Add sufficient egg to bind and create a firm mixture.

3. Dampen your hands and roll heaped tablespoonfuls of the mixture into 24 evenly-sized balls.

4. Arrange the meatballs on a lined baking sheet.

5. Drizzle the meatballs with sunflower oil and bake in the preheated oven for 15 minutes, until beginning to brown and cooked through. You will need to turn the meatballs halfway through cooking.

6. In the meantime, prepare the glaze. Add the ketchup, garlic, paprika, soy sauce, sherry vinegar, butter, and brown sugar to a pan, and while frequently stirring, bring to simmer. Cook for approximately 5 minutes until the mixture begins to thicken and become glossy.

7. Pour approximately half of the glaze over the meatballs and roll them around to ensure they are evenly coated before returning them to the oven for 5 minutes.

8. When you are ready to serve, pop a cocktail stick into each meatball and place on a serving platter.

9. Serve with any remaining ketchup glaze.

Prawn Cocktail

A quintessentially British Christmas Day appetizer, this prawn cocktail just wouldn't be the same without the ketchup-based sauce!

Servings: 4

Total Time: 40mins

Ingredients:

- Squeeze of fresh lemon juice
- Glug of malt vinegar
- 20 raw shell-on tiger prawns
- 1 little gem lettuce
- Spring of fresh thyme (leaves picked)
- Cayenne pepper (to garnish)
- Freshly squeezed juice of ½ a lemon
- 1 tbsp Worcestershire sauce
- 5 tbsp tomato ketchup
- ½ tsp smokey paprika
- Splash of Tabasco sauce
- ½ tsp sweet paprika
- 1 tbsp double cream
- 4 tbsp full-fat mayonnaise
- Pinch of cayenne
- Pinch of sea salt
- 1 tsp cracked black pepper

Directions:

1. Bring a deep saucepan of water to a boil. Stir in a squeeze of fresh lemon juice and a good glug of malt vinegar.

2. Add the prawns to the boiling water and cook until they float to the surface of the water. Drain well and chill in a bowl of icy-cold water.

3. Remove the cool prawns from the bowl and carefully peel. You will need 1 prawn left whole per serving, to garnish.

4. Slice the lettuce in half and place in a bowl of icy-cold water, until crisped.

5. To make the sauce: In a bowl, combine the lemon juice, with the Worcestershire sauce, tomato ketchup, smokey paprika, a splash of Tabasco, sweet paprika, double cream mayonnaise, a pinch of cayenne, a pinch of sea salt and black pepper. Stir well to incorporate.

6. To serve: Drain the lettuce and using kitchen paper towel, pat dry.

7. Arrange ⅔ of the lettuce leaves in Martini glasses.

8. Julienne the remaining lettuce leaves and add them to a large bowl.

9. Add the peeled prawns, along with a spoonful of the sauce.

10. Top with the unpeeled whole prawn, and a scattering of cayenne pepper.

11. Enjoy.

Shrimp Pasta Salad

Featuring juicy, bite-sized shrimp tossed in a tangy dressing makes an excellent seafood-based pasta lite bite.

Servings: 12

Total Time: 30mins

Ingredients:

- 1 pound package ditalini (small thimble) pasta
- 1½ cups frozen cooked baby shrimp (thawed)
- 1½ cups English cucumber (diced)
- 1 large tomato (diced)

Dressing:

- 1¼ cups mayonnaise
- 2-3 tbsp ketchup
- 1½ tsp salt
- 1½ tsp sugar
- 1 tbsp horseradish
- 1-2 tsp milk (as needed)
- Salt and black pepper (to season)

Directions:

1. Cook the pasta according to the package directions and until al dente. Drain thoroughly and run under cold water until cooled. Drain once more and transfer to a large bowl.

2. Drain and thoroughly rinse the shrimp under cool water. Add to the pasta along with the cucumber and tomatoes. Put to one side.

3. Next, prepare the dressing. In a bowl, whisk the mayonnaise with the ketchup, salt, sugar, and horseradish. Add the milk a little at a time until you achieve your desired consistency.

4. Pour the dressing over the pasta and stir to combine, to evenly coat.

5. Season with salt and pepper.

6. Chill the pasta salad until you are ready to serve.

Toasted Reubens

This tasty toasted lite-bite is ready to enjoy in no time at all making it ideal for anyone having a busy day.

Servings: 4

Total Time: 15mins

Ingredients:

- 4 tsp prepared mustard
- 8 slices rye bread
- 4 slices Swiss cheese
- 1 pound deli corned beef (thinly sliced)
- 1 (8 ounce) can sauerkraut (rinsed, drained)
- ½ cup mayonnaise
- 3 tbsp ketchup
- 2 tbsp sweet pickle relish
- 1 tbsp prepared horseradish
- 2 tbsp butter

Directions:

1. Evenly spread the mustard over 4 slices of bread.

2. Layer the bread with cheese, corned beef, and sauerkraut.

3. In a small-size bowl, mix the mayonnaise with the ketchup, sweet pickle relish, and horseradish.

4. Spread the mayonnaise mixture over the remaining slices of bread.

5. Place the bread over the sauerkraut.

6. Spread the outside of the sandwiches with butter.

7. In a large frying pan, over moderate heat, cook the sandwiches for 3-4 minutes, on each side until golden and the cheese entirely melted.

8. Serve.

Mains

BBQ Mac n' Cheese

Transform classic mac n' cheese into a new and exciting meal with a deliciously tangy tomato BBQ sauce.

Servings: 6

Total Time: 40mins

Ingredients:

- 1 pound macaroni
- ½ cup Parmesan cheese
- 1 cup cottage cheese
- 1¼ cups milk
- ½ cup ketchup
- ½ jalapeno
- 1 tsp brown sugar
- 3 garlic cloves (peeled)
- ½ cup fresh parsley
- ½ tsp salt
- ½ tsp black pepper
- ¾ tsp ground cumin
- 2-3 tbsp butter
- ¼ cup Italian-style breadcrumbs
- 1 cup Cheddar cheese (shredded, divided)
- 1 onion (peeled, diced)

Directions:

1. Prepare the macaroni according to the package instructions. Drain and put to one side.

2. In a food processor, combine the Parmesan, cottage cheese, milk, ketchup, jalapeno, brown sugar, garlic, fresh parsley, salt, pepper, and cumin.

3. Heat a frying pan and add the butter to melt.

4. Sauté the onions in the butter until translucent and softened.

5. Heat a skillet with butter, and add the breadcrumbs, tossing to brown.

6. Preheat the main oven to 325 degrees F.

7. Lightly butter a casserole dish.

8. Add the drained macaroni to the dish followed by the cottage cheese mixture, ¾ cup of shredded Cheddar, and diced onion. Toss to combine.

9. Top with the breadcrumbs, a few knobs of butter, and the remaining shredded cheese.

10. Bake in the preheated oven for 25-30 minutes, until golden.

Catfish Stew

Catfish is a very underrated source of protein, and this main meal is flavorful and filling.

Servings: 4-6

Total Time: 1hour 10mins

Ingredients:

- ½ pound thick-cut bacon (cut into ½" pieces)
- 1 medium-size onion (peeled, finely diced)
- ½ cup celery (finely diced)
- 1 (14 ounce) can petite diced tomatoes (undrained)
- 1 cup fish stock
- 3 tbsp ketchup
- 1 tbsp Worcestershire sauce
- 1 tsp salt
- ½ tsp black pepper
- ½ tsp thyme
- ½ tsp red pepper flakes
- 3 medium-size potatoes (peeled, diced)
- 1 pound catfish fillets

Directions:

1. Over moderately high heat, brown the bacon in a Dutch oven until crisp.

2. Add the onions and celery and sauté until the onions are tender, for 3-5 minutes.

3. Add the tomatoes along with the fish stock, ketchup, Worcestershire sauces, salt, black pepper, thyme, red pepper flakes, and potatoes. Stir thoroughly to combine.

4. Add sufficient water to the pot until the potatoes are fully submerged. Bring to boil, before reducing to moderately low heat. Cover with a lid and cook for 20-30 minutes, until the potatoes are fork-tender.

5. Add the catfish, cover with a lid, and continue to cook for 10 minutes. Taste for seasoning and add salt and black pepper if necessary.

6. Remove from the heat, cover with a lid, and allow the stew to rest for 15-20 minutes before serving.

Chickpea Ketchup Curry

Looking for a meat-free curry? Then you have come to the right place, this chickpea curry is healthy, and packed with flavor.

Servings: 2

Total Time: 25mins

Ingredients:

- 2 tbsp sunflower oil
- 1 small-size onion (peeled, thinly sliced)
- ¾" piece of ginger (peeled, finely grated)
- Pinch of dried chili flakes
- 1 clove garlic (peeled, crushed)
- 2 tsp curry powder
- 1 (14 ounce) can chickpeas (drained)
- 5 tbsp tomato ketchup
- Freshly squeezed juice of ½ lemon
- Salt and black pepper
- Basmati rice (to serve, optional)
- Coriander (chopped, to serve)

Directions:

1. Over moderate-low heat, heat the oil.

2. Add the onions to the pan and sweat for 7-8 minutes, until golden and softened.

3. Stir in the ginger followed by the chili flakes, garlic, and curry powder. Fry for an additional 2 minutes, while constantly stirring.

4. Next, add the chickpeas along with the ketchup and sufficient water to thicken or thin out the consistency of the sauce.

5. Gently simmer for 5 minutes.

6. Stir in the freshly squeezed lemon juice and season with salt and black pepper.

7. Serve with rice and garnish with chopped coriander.

Cola Chicken

Cola Chicken is good to go from pan to plate in under 30 minutes. It can't be bad. Serve with rice for a healthy and tasty meal that your children will love too.

Servings: 4

Total Time: 35mins

Ingredients:

- 2 tbsp canola oil
- ½ cup onion (peeled, chopped)
- 4 (4 ounce) boneless skinless chicken breast halves
- 1 (12 ounce) can cola (any brand)
- 1 cup ketchup
- ⅛ tsp garlic powder
- ⅛ tsp salt
- ⅛ tsp pepper
- 4½ tsp cornstarch
- 3 tbsp cold water

Directions:

1. In a frying pan, in oil, sauté the onion until fork-tender.

2. Add the chicken to the pan and brown on all sides.

3. Pour in the cola and add the ketchup followed by the garlic powder, salt, and black pepper.

4. Cover the pan with a lid and simmer for approximately 25-30 minutes, or until a meat thermometer inserted into the thickest part of the meat registers 170 degrees F.

5. Remove the chicken and keep warm.

6. In a bowl, combine the cornstarch with the cold water until smooth. Gradually add the slurry to the pan and bring to boil. Cook while stirring for a couple of minutes to thicken.

7. Return the chicken to the pan and heat through before serving.

Crab Hash

Forget the corned beef - this crab hash is a savory main to enjoy with poached or fried eggs.

Servings: 4

Total Time: 40mins

Ingredients:

- 2 tbsp olive oil
- 1 large-size onion (peeled, cut into ½" dice)
- 1 (16 ounce) can claw crab (picked over)
- 1½ pounds Idaho potatoes (peeled, cut into ½" dice)
- 2 tbsp olive oil
- 2 tbsp ketchup
- 1 tbsp Dijon mustard
- ½ tsp Old Bay seasoning
- 2 tbsp fresh basil (chopped)
- 2 tbsp water
- Salt and freshly ground black pepper
- Poached of fried eggs (to serve, optional)

Directions:

1. In a 12" skillet or frying pan, over low heat, heat 2 tablespoons of olive oil.

2. Increase the heat to moderate to high, and once the oil begins to smoke, add the onion along with the crab and while frequently stirring, cook for 4-6 minutes, or until golden.

3. Transfer the crab mixture to a bowl and set aside.

4. Toss the diced potatoes with the remaining oil.

5. Add the potatoes to the 12" skillet or frying pan and while occasionally stirring cook, for 10 minutes, until they have a golden crust.

6. While the potatoes cook, in a bowl, combine the ketchup with the mustard, Old Bay seasoning, basil, and 2 tablespoons of water.

7. Return the crab mixture set aside in Step 3 to the skillet. Add the ketchup mixture and stir to combine.

8. Season with salt and black pepper and continue to cook while frequently stirring until the hash is browned; this will take approximately 5 minutes.

9. Serve topped with poached or fried eggs.

Grilled Lamb Chops with Pineapple

Grilling fruit to serve alongside meat is a great way to pep up an otherwise ordinary main. So next time you are in the farmer's market or store, make sure to pick up a pineapple!

Servings: 6

Total Time: 45mins

Ingredients:

Marinade:

- 2 tbsp currant jam
- 2 tbsp ketchup
- 2 tbsp soy sauce
- 2 tbsp brown sugar
- 1 tbsp dry mustard
- 2 tsp Worcestershire sauce

Chops:

- 3 pounds lamb loin chops (cut 1" thick and fat trimmed)
- 6 (½" thick) slices of pineapple

Directions:

1. In a bowl, combine the currant jam with the ketchup, soy sauce, brown sugar, dry mustard, and Worcestershire sauce.

2. Add the chops to a large ziplock bag.

3. Pour the marinade into the bag and seal.

4. Place the bag in the fridge for 15 minutes to marinate. Do not leave for longer as this will mask the flavor of the meat.

5. Take the lamb bout of the bag, shake off any excess marinade. Discard the bag along with the marinade.

6. Arrange the lamb and the slice of pineapple in the middle of a cooking grate.

7. Grill the pineapple for 5-7 minutes, until grill marks appear. You will need to flip the slices over once during grilling.

8. For rare, grill the chops for 7-9 minutes (140 degrees F), 10-12 minutes for medium doneness (160 degrees F), and 13-15 minutes, for medium to well done (170 degrees F). Flip the chops over halfway through the grilling time.

9. Serve the lamb with the grilled pineapple and enjoy!

Japanese-Style Ketchup Spaghetti

When time is short, this ketchup spaghetti will save the day. The kids will love it too.

Servings: 2

Total Time: 30mins

Ingredients:

- 7 ounces spaghetti
- 2 tbsp extra-virgin olive oil
- 1 garlic clove (peeled, minced)
- ½ onion (peeled, sliced)
- 2 Italian sausages (sliced)
- 1 bell pepper (sliced)
- 4-6 mushrooms (sliced)
- 2 tbsp milk
- 2 tbsp Parmesan cheese (freshly ground)
- 4 tbsp ketchup
- 1 tsp Worcestershire sauce
- ¼ tsp sugar
- 1-3 tbsp reserved pasta cooking liquid
- Sea salt
- Freshly ground black pepper

Directions:

1. Bring a large pan of salted water to boil and cook the spaghetti according to the package instructions, until al dente. Drain and set aside. Reserve 1-3 tablespoon of the pasta cooking liquid.

2. In the meantime, over moderate heat, in a frying pan, heat the oil.

3. Add the garlic to the pan and sauté for 60 seconds until it emits its fragrance and is golden.

4. Add the onions to the pan and sauté for 2-3 minutes, until wilted.

5. Next, add the sausage and fry for 60 seconds.

6. Add the bell pepper and mushrooms to the pan and sauté until cooked through.

7. For the sauce, stir in the ketchup, Worcestershire sauce, reserved pasta cooking liquid, and sugar.

8. Season with a pinch of salt, and a dash of pepper

9. Add the drained pasta to the pan and toss with kitchen tongs to combine and heat through.

10. Stir in the milk and cheese and toss to coat and combine evenly.

11. Serve and enjoy.

Ketchup Shrimp

Ketchup is often used in Chinese cooking, and garlic and ketchup are the perfect pairing of flavors and never more so than when used to cook juicy shrimp.

Servings: 2

Total Time: 30mins

Ingredients:

- 1 cup oil
- 14 ounces shrimp (deveined, headed, washed, patted dry)
- 1 tbsp garlic (peeled, minced)
- 1 tbsp ginger (peeled, minced)
- 2 scallions (white and green parts separated)
- 1½ tbsp ketchup
- ½ cup warm chicken broth
- 1 tsp sugar
- 1 tbsp reduced-salt soy sauce
- 1 tbsp Shaoxing wine
- Salt (to season)
- Rice (to serve, optional)

Directions:

1. In a deep-sided pan, heat the oil until very hot.

2. Add the shrimp to the pan, and quickly fry until they become red.

3. Transfer the shrimp to a plate and pour off all but 1 tbsp of the oil.

4. Add the garlic, ginger, and scallions to the pan and over low heat, cook until fragrant.

5. Next, stir in the ketchup and chicken broth. Mix to combine.

6. Return the shrimp to the pan and add the sugar, soy sauce, and wine. Continue to cook for 2-3 minutes or until the sauce is thickened and adhering to the shrimp.

7. Taste and season with salt.

8. Serve on a bed of rice.

Meatloaf

After a long day at school or work, nothing beats a homemade meatloaf.

Servings: 8-10

Total Time: 1hour 40mins

Ingredients:

- Nonstick cooking spray
- 1 large onion (peeled, finely chopped)
- ¼ cup Italian dressing
- 1½ pounds extra-lean ground beef
- ¾ cup tomato ketchup (divided)
- 4¼ ounces low-salt, stovetop chicken stuffing mix
- ¾ cup water
- 2 egg whites
- ½ cup mature Cheddar cheese (shredded)

Directions:

1. Preheat the main oven to 375 degrees F. Spritz a 13x9" baking dish with nonstick cooking spray.

2. Over moderate heat, in a pan, cook the onions in the Italian dressing until golden and while frequently stirring. Remove the pan from the heat and allow to cool.

3. In a bowl, combine the beef with the onions, ¼ cup of ketchup, stuffing mix, water, and egg white. Mix to incorporate.

4. Using clean hands, shape the mixture into a 10x5" loaf shake and place in the preached baking dish. Cover the meatloaf with the reaming ketchup.

5. Bake in the preheated oven for 60 minutes, or until the meatloaf registers an internal temperature of 160 degrees F.

6. Top with shredded Cheddar and bake for an additional 2-3 minutes, until the cheese is entirely melted.

Root Beer Glazed Chicken

Cheer up chicken with a root beer, mustard, and ketchup glaze for a fast and flavorful family meal.

Servings: 4

Total Time: 20mins

Ingredients:

- 4 (6 ounce) boneless skinless chicken breast halves (slightly flattened)
- 2 tbsp canola oil
- 1 cup root beer
- ½ cup packed brown sugar
- ¼ cup ketchup
- 4 tsp Dijon mustard
- 2 tsp lemon zest (grated)

Directions:

1. In a large frying pan, cook the chicken in the canola oil until an internal meat thermometer registers 170 degrees F. this will take approximately 4-6 minutes on each side. Remove the chicken from the pan and keep warm.

2. Pour in the root beer and add the brown sugar, ketchup, mustard, and lemon zest. Stir to combine and bring to boil. Continue to cook while stirring for 6-8 minutes, or until thickened.

3. Return the chicken o the pan and cook until heated through.

4. Serve and enjoy.

Shepherd's Pie

Shepherd's Pie is the epitome of comfort food. A well-loved main course in the UK it is typically served with seasonal veggies.

Servings: 6

Total Time: 1hour 15mins

Ingredients:

- 4 large potatoes (peeled, cubed)
- 1 tbsp butter
- 1 tbsp onion (peeled, finely chopped)
- ¼ cup Cheddar cheese (shredded)
- Salt and black pepper
- 5 carrots (chopped)
- 1 tbsp vegetable oil
- 1 onion (peeled, chopped)
- 1 pound lean ground beef
- 2 tbsp all-purpose flour
- 1 tbsp ketchup
- ¾ beef broth
- ¼ Cheddar cheese (shredded)

Directions:

1. Bring a large pan of salted water to boil.

2. Add the potatoes to the pan and cook for 15 minutes, until firm but fork tender - drain and mash.

3. Add the butter to the mash along with the chopped onion and ¼ cup of shredded Cheddar — season to taste and put to one side.

4. Bring a large pan of salted water to boil and add the carrots, cooking until bite-tender, for approximately 15 minutes. Drain, mash, and put to one side.

5. Preheat the main oven to 375 degrees F.

6. In a large frying pan, heat the oil.

7. Add the onion and cook until clear.

8. Next, add the beef and cook until browned.

9. Pour off any excess fat and stir in the flour - cook for 60 seconds.

10. Add the ketchup followed by the beef broth. Bring to boil before reducing to simmer. Simmer for 5 minutes.

11. Spread the beef in an even layer on the bottom of a 2-quart baking dish.

12. Next, spread a layer of mashed carrots.

13. Top with the potato mash and scatter over the remaining Cheddar cheese.

14. Bake in the preheated oven for approximately 20-25 minutes, until golden.

15. Serve with seasonal veggies.

Slow Cooker Pork Chops

Cook these tasty pork chops low and slow for a hassle-free midweek or weekend family meal.

Servings: 4

Total Time: 4hours 15mins

Ingredients:

- 1 tsp garlic powder
- ½ tsp salt
- ¼ tsp black pepper
- 4 (8 ounce) bone-in pork loin chops
- 2 cups ketchup
- ½ cup packed brown sugar
- 1 tsp liquid smoke

Directions:

1. In a bowl, combine the garlic powder with the salt and pepper and sprinkle the seasoning over the pork chops.

2. In a large frying pan, combine the ketchup with the brown sugar, and liquid smoke.

3. Pour half of the sauce into a slow cooker of 3-quart capacity.

4. Top with the chops and the remaining sauce.

5. Cover and on low cook for 4-5 hours, until the pork is tender.

6. Serve.

Sweet and Savory Brisket

Serve with seasonal veggies and mash potatoes or slice and use as a sandwich filler. Either way, this beef dish is extremely flavorful.

Servings: 10

Total Time: 8hours 20mins

Ingredients:

- 1 (3-3½ pound) beef brisket (halved)
- 1 cup ketchup
- 1 sachet onion flavor soup mix
- ¼ cup grape jelly
- ½ tsp black pepper

Directions:

1. Arrange half of the brisket in a slow cooker of 5-quart capacity.

2. In a bowl, combine the ketchup with the onion soup mix, jelly, and black pepper. Spread half the mixture over the brisket half.

3. Top with the remaining half of brisket. Spread the remaining ketchup mixture over the top.

4. Cover and on low, cook for 8-10 hours, or until the meat is fork-tender.

5. Slice and serve with any cooking juices.

Teriyaki Salmon with Ketchup

Ketchup is often used in Asian cooking, and this Teriyaki Salmon is perfect for anyone watching their weight.

Servings: 2

Total Time: 15mins

Ingredients:

- 2 (2½ ounce) salmon fillets (cut into chunks)
- Pinch of salt
- Dash of pepper
- Flour
- Splash of oil
- 2 tbsp ketchup
- ½ tsp soy sauce
- ½ tsp mirin
- ½ tsp sugar (optional)
- ½ tsp water
- 4 lettuce leaves
- 4 cherry tomatoes

Directions:

1. Season the fish with salt and pepper.

2. Pat away any excess moisture from the surface of each fillet and lightly cover in flour.

3. Add the oil to a frying pan, and over moderately high heat, fry the fish on both sides for a total of 4 minutes.

4. Reduce the heat to moderate to low and continue to cook until the fish flakes easily when using a fork and is cooked through.

5. Add the ketchup, soy sauce, mirin, sugar, and water to the pan, and mix to combine.

6. Arrange each fillet on 2 lettuce leaves and top with cherry tomatoes.

Sauces, Dips 'n Sides

Baked Beans

Your family will love this simple side of beans to serve with burgers, hot dogs, or any type of grilled meat.

Servings: 6

Total Time: 20

Ingredients:

- 2 (14½ ounce) cans pork and beans
- 2 tbsp ketchup
- 1 tbsp Worcestershire sauce
- 1 tbsp yellow mustard
- 2 tbsp packed brown sugar
- 3 tbsp bacon bits
- ¼ cup onion (peeled, chopped)

Directions:

1. Add the beans, ketchup, Worcestershire sauce, mustard, brown sugar, bacon bits and onion to a microwave-safe dish of 1½ quart capacity. Stir to combine.

2. On high, microwave for 6 minutes.

3. Stir and microwave for an additional 2 minutes, or until hot.

4. Set aside to stand for a couple of minutes.

5. Stir and serve.

Burger Sauce

It's far better to make your own burger sauce. Not only is it less expensive but also it's a lot healthier.

Servings: 10

Total Time: 35mins

Ingredients:

- 1 cup mayonnaise
- 1 cup tomato ketchup
- ¼ cup sweet relish (any brand)
- 1 tbsp apple cider vinegar
- 2 tsp sugar
- 2 cloves of garlic (peeled, minced)
- ⅛ tsp pepper

Directions:

1. In a bowl, combine the mayonnaise with the ketchup, relish, vinegar, sugar, garlic, and pepper.

2. Transfer to the fridge for half an hour and serve.

Caramelized Garlic and Onion Ketchup

This ketchup is delicious served with grilled meat, burgers, or hot dogs.

Servings: 6

Total Time: 40mins

Ingredients:

- 1 tbsp oil
- ½ cup onions (peeled, chopped)
- 1 tsp chipotle chili pepper powder
- 3 garlic cloves (peeled, minced)
- Freshly ground black pepper
- 1½ cups tomato ketchup

Directions:

1. Over moderate heat, in a small frying pan, heat the oil.

2. Add the onions and chili pepper powder to the pan and simmer over moderate-low heat for 10 minutes, while occasionally stirring.

3. Add the garlic to the pan and cook for an additional 5 minutes, until the onions are golden.

4. Allow to cool.

5. Spoon the onion mixture into a bowl, season with ground black pepper and stir in the ketchup.

6. Mix well to combine and serve.

Catalina Dressing

This dressing hails from the 1960s but proves the age-old saying that the oldies are the besties!

Servings: 10-12

Total times: 15mins

Ingredients:

- ½ cup ketchup
- ½ cup sugar
- ½ cup red wine vinegar
- ½ cup onion (peeled, grated)
- 1 tsp paprika
- ½ tsp Worcestershire sauce
- 1 cup salad oil
- Salt and pepper

Directions:

1. In a food processor, combine the ketchup with the sugar, vinegar, onion, paprika, and Worcestershire sauce. On pulse, process until blended.

2. While the processor is still running, gradually pour in the oil.

3. Taste and season.

4. Cover and place in the fridge until needed.

Comeback Sauce

Comeback sauce is a popular Southern dipping sauce. It's ideal for chips, fries, veggies, seafood, onion rings, and chicken.

Servings: 4-6

Total Time: 8hours 10mins

Ingredients:

- 1¼ cups mayonnaise
- ¼ cup chili sauce
- ¼ cup tomato ketchup
- 1 tbsp freshly squeezed lemon juice
- 2 tsp Worcestershire sauce
- 1 tsp garlic salt
- 1 tsp smoked paprika
- 1 tsp hot sauce
- ½ tsp onion powder

Directions:

1. Add the mayonnaise, chili sauce, ketchup, lemon juice, Worcestershire sauce, garlic salt, smoked paprika hot sauce, and onion powder to a bowl and whisk until entirely combined.

2. Transfer to an airtight resealable container in the fridge overnight.

3. Serve as needed.

Curry Ketchup

Add tangy lime juice and hot curry powder to tomato ketchup and give some spicy and zest to America's favorite condiment.

Servings: 4

Total Time: 5mins

Ingredients:

- ½ cup ketchup
- 1½ tsp freshly squeezed lime juice
- ½ tsp curry powder

Directions:

1. In a bowl, combine the ketchup with the freshly squeezed lime juice and curry powder. Stir to incorporate.

2. Store in the fridge for up to 21 days in a resealable container.

3. Use as needed.

Honey Apple Barbecue Sauce

Give grilled chicken a makeover with this homemade sauce.

Servings: 16

Total Time: 10mins

Ingredients:

- 1 cup tomato ketchup
- 1 cup applesauce
- 2 tbsp honey
- ¼ tsp ground cinnamon

Directions:

1. Add the ketchup, applesauce, honey, and cinnamon to a pan and on moderate-low heat simmer for 5 minutes, while occasionally stirring.

2. Allow to cool.

3. Place in the fridge until you are ready to serve.

Hot Reuben Dip

Serve this hot dip at your next get-together or party and enjoy with rye bread, crackers or crisps.

Servings: 8

Total Time: 30mins

Ingredients:

- 8 ounces cream cheese
- 1 cup mayonnaise
- 2 tbsp ketchup
- 3 tsp sweet pickle relish
- 2 cups sauerkraut (well-drained)
- 16 ounces Swiss cheese (diced small)
- 8 ounces corned beef (shredded)
- Chives (thinly sliced, to garnish)
- Rye bread (to serve)
- Crackers (to serve)
- Crisps (to garnish)

Directions:

1. Preheat the main oven to 350 degrees F.

2. With a mixer, mix the cream cheese with the mayonnaise and ketchup.

3. By hand, stir in the relish followed by the sauerkraut, Swiss cheese, and corned beef.

4. Taste, and adjust the seasoning, add additional ketchup if needed.

5. Transfer to an ovenproof casserole dish and bake in the oven for 15-20 minutes, until the surface is beginning to brown, and the dip bubbling around the edges and the cheese entirely melted.

6. Garnish with sliced chives, and serve warm with rye bread, crackers or crisps.

North Carolina Red Coleslaw

Using tomato ketchup rather than mayonnaise for this creamy coleslaw will give it its red color while the hot sauce adds a touch of heat.

Servings: 10-12

Total Time: 35mins

Ingredients:

Dressing:

- ⅔ cup apple cider vinegar
- ½ cup tomato ketchup
- ¼ cup sugar
- 2 tsp freshly ground black pepper
- 2 tsp hot sauce

Slaw:

- 1 large head green cabbage (finely shredded)
- 1 large-size carrot (peeled, grated on large holes)
- ⅓ cup sea salt

Directions:

1. To prepare the dressing: In a small bowl, whisk the apple cider vinegar with the tomato ketchup, sugar, black pepper, and hot sauce.

2. For the slaw: In a large bowl, combine the shredded cabbage with the carrots. Scatter with the sugar and salt and toss to combine evenly. Set aside to stand for 5 minutes before transferring to a colander and rinsing thoroughly under cold running tap water.

3. Place the veggies in a salad spinner and spin dry. Alternatively, blot with kitchen paper towels. Return to the large bowl.

4. Pour the dressing over the veggies and toss to coat evenly.

5. Taste and season with additional salt, black pepper or sugar, as needed.

6. Serve.

Pineapple and Brown Sugar BBQ Sauce

Give pork, beef, or pork a makeover with this fruity BBQ sauce. It's surprisingly easy to make but can transform a good meal into a great one.

Servings: 30

Total Time: 20mins

Ingredients:

- ¾ cup packed brown sugar
- 1 cup pineapple juice
- ½ tsp garlic
- 2 tbsp Worcestershire sauce
- ¾ cup ketchup
- Pinch of red pepper flakes
- ½ tsp onion powder
- Pinch of salt
- 1-2 tbsp cornstarch
- 1-2 tbsp water

Directions:

1. Add the brown sugar, pineapple juice, Worcestershire sauce, garlic, ketchup, red pepper flakes, onion powder, and salt to a pan. Bring to boil before reducing o moderate-low heat and simmering for 10-15 minutes, until the flavors infuse.

2. Ina cup mix equal amounts of cornstarch and water and mix to combine.

3. Slowly add the slurry to the sauce while stirring until thickened.

4. Serve.

Red Remoulade

Serve this remoulade on roast beef sandwiches or as a topping for crisp French fries or seafood.

Servings: 6-8

Total Time: 2hours 10mins

Ingredients:

- 1 cup ketchup
- ½ cup extra-virgin olive oil
- ¼ cup Creole or whole grain mustard
- ¼ cup freshly squeezed lemon juice
- ½ cup celery (finely chopped)
- ½ cup green onion (finely chopped)
- ½ cup Italian parsley (finely chopped)
- 2 cloves garlic (peeled, finely chopped)
- 2 tbsp paprika
- 2 tsp Worcestershire sauce
- ½ tsp salt
- Splash of Tabasco

Directions:

1. In a bowl, combine the ketchup with the oil, Creole mustard, lemon juice, celery, green onions, parsley, garlic, paprika, Worcestershire sauce, and salt. Stir until thoroughly mixed.

2. Transfer to the fridge, covered, for 2-3 hours to allow the flavors to intensify.

3. Taste and season just before serving.

Spiced Cranberry Ketchup

Warm spices will add depth of flavor to regular tomato ketchup while cranberries will provide texture.

Servings: 4

Total Time: 5mins

Ingredients:

- ½ cup ketchup
- 2 tbsp frozen or fresh cranberries (chopped)
- 1 tsp ground cinnamon
- 1 tsp ground nutmeg
- 1 tsp ground allspice

Directions:

1. In a bowl, combine the ketchup with the cranberries, cinnamon, nutmeg, and allspice.

2. Transfer to a resealable container and place in the fridge for up to 21 days.

3. Serve as needed.

Strawberry Ketchup

Tomatoes are a fruit, so it makes perfect sense to pair them with another, and here strawberry preserves add intense sweetness to regular ketchup.

Servings: 2-4

Total Time: 5mins

Ingredients:

- ½ cup ketchup
- 3 tbsp strawberry preserves
- 1 tbsp freshly squeezed lemon juice
- ¼ tsp onion powder

Directions:

1. In a mixing bowl, combine the ketchup with the strawberry preserves, fresh lemon juice, and onion powder. Stir well to incorporate.

2. Serve or store, covered in the fridge for up to 4 days.

Sweet and Sour Sauce

No Chinese feast is complete without this staple sauce. Use it for dipping, glazing, or to pour over meat and veggies.

Servings: 6

Total Time: 10mins

Ingredients:

- ½ cup tomato ketchup
- ⅓ cup rice wine vinegar
- ⅓ cup packed brown sugar
- 1 tsp soy sauce
- ¼ tsp powdered ginger
- 1 cup water (divided)
- 3 tbsp cornstarch

Directions:

1. In a pan, whisk the ketchup with the rice wine vinegar, brown sugar, soy sauce, powdered ginger, and ¾ cup of water. Bring to boil while whisking.

2. Turn the heat down to low and allow the mixture to simmer for 3 minutes.

3. In a cup, dissolve the cornstarch in the remaining ¼ cup of water and whisk until silky smooth.

4. Add the slurry to the pan and whisk to incorporate.

5. Continue to whisk and cook the sauce over low heat for 2-3 minutes, or until thickened.

6. Store, covered in the fridge.

Author's Afterthoughts

thank you

I would like to express my deepest thanks to you, the reader, for making this investment in one my books. I cherish the thought of bringing the love of cooking into your home.

With so much choice out there, I am grateful you decided to Purch this book and read it from beginning to end.

Please let me know by submitting an Amazon review if you enjoyed this book and found it contained valuable information to help you in your culinary endeavors. Please take a few minutes to express your opinion freely and honestly. This will help others make an informed decision on purchasing and provide me with valuable feedback.

Thank you for taking the time to review!

Christina Tosch

About the Author

Christina Tosch is a successful chef and renowned cookbook author from Long Grove, Illinois. She majored in Liberal Arts at Trinity International University and decided to pursue her passion of cooking when she applied to the world renowned Le Cordon Bleu culinary school in Paris, France. The school was lucky to recognize the immense talent of this chef and she excelled in her courses, particularly Haute Cuisine. This skill was recognized and rewarded by several highly regarded Chicago restaurants, where she was offered the prestigious position of head chef.

Christina and her family live in a spacious home in the Chicago area and she loves to grow her own vegetables and herbs in the garden she lovingly cultivates on her sprawling estate. Her and her husband have two beautiful children, 3 cats, 2 dogs and a parakeet they call Jasper. When Christina is not hard at work creating beautiful meals for Chicago's elite, she is hard at work writing engaging e-books of which she has sold over 1500.

Make sure to keep an eye out for her latest books that offer helpful tips, clear instructions and witty anecdotes that will bring a smile to your face as you read!